FROM UNDER THE HOOD: THERAPY TWINS' GUIDE TO A SMOOTHER RIDE

Narrated by Change,
Navigated by Jane and Joan

THERAPY TWINS

Co-editor Dallas Kalmar

BALBOA
PRESS
A DIVISION OF HAY HOUSE

Balboa Press books may be ordered through booksellers or by contacting:

Balboa Press
A Division of Hay House
1663 Liberty Drive
Bloomington, IN 47403
www.balboapress.com
1 (877) 407-4847

Print information available on the last page.

ISBN: 978-1-5043-8229-8 (sc)
ISBN: 978-1-5043-8228-1 (e)

Library of Congress Control Number: 2017911220

Balboa Press rev. date: 08/03/2017

Contents

Acknowledgments

Of course, we thank our family because everyone else does. If we didn't, they'd have the mob after us. We thank our parents for their resiliency, lifting the family out of poverty to the illusion of middle class. And, of course, our sister, Lori, who maintains the happy-ending fairy tale as her motto.

There are many others we could and do thank, but as Steve Perry says, "The list goes on and on and on ..."

We'd also like to thank this book because it has served as a vehicle for our own healing.

We would like to extend our deepest Love & acknowledgement to our sister Lori "Mothers Little Helper" who finally turned us on to a self-help book we were not only able to read, but also jump started our engines!!

We'd like to extend our heartfelt gratitude to Dallas Kalmar for her creative ideas and meticulous writing styles that transformed our visions 'From Under The Hood'

Foreword

Hello, My name is Evie
Rita is my Twin
Early August 1960
I gave birth to TherapyTwins

Antisocial by Nature
They didn't approve of Company
Not the Milkman
Not the Mailman
Not even Uncle Ralph

But who would have Guessed

TherapyTwins
Didn't make a Sound
When Firefighters barged In
Black boots, black hats, & Axes
TherapyTwins just Grinned

Threw rocks at Cars
Were Brownies for a Day
Could sit for Hours
By Night and by Day

Who would Think
TherapyTwins would grow Up
To help so Many

So fasten your Seat-belt
Enjoy the Ride
Let TherapyTwins
Blow your Mind

Love Mom

How to Use This "Manual"

Designed to be more of a survival guide in a cliff notes kind of way, *From Under the Hood* is not your typical self-help book. Lord knows we've sifted through hundreds of them, throwing most of them away and many across the room.

Sound familiar? If so, we implore you not to do what we did, which was to use the remaining books for anything but reading (for example, portable coffee tables, window-proppers, writing surfaces, and dining tables for our cats). We hoped they might help us just by being there, or through osmosis.

Instead, we feel anyone could benefit from reading this or any self-help book cover to cover. Our suggestion for those of you who are short on time (or with short attention spans, like us) is to flip a book open and read whatever that page or section has to offer you. Odds are, the message found will be exactly what you need at that juncture.

So by letting our hair down and coughing up some of our own failure and success stories with a dash of humor, we offer you a unique opportunity to learn how to transform into a new and improved you. So, hitch a ride with Therapy Twins® on a journey of self-awareness. Learn how to follow in our sister Lori's, footsteps and trade in your current situation for the life of your dreams.

One more thing. As you read, keep this in mind: the mind is the steering wheel of the brain. No worries if you don't understand yet. We'll explain later.

Introduction

"All who joy would win must share it.
Happiness was born a twin."
—Lord Byron (1788–1824)

Well, that wasn't always the case for us, Jane and Joan. Born premature identical twins in the sixties, given our last rights, and named by the nurses, it was thought we wouldn't survive—but we did.

Thrust into life, we landed just as quickly into separate incubators. This was the time when hospital staff provided the only human touch premature infants received. Joan happened to be sicker and weaker than Jane. As she was being poked and prodded, developing a quick startle reflex, Jane was wheeled to a corner, promptly becoming a tiny expert in dissociation. Joan was born with a brain tumor, requiring major surgery at the teeny age of six months. Since neither twin was ever sure where her twin was during those formative weeks of development, it's no wonder Joan grew up quite anxious and Jane with symptoms of depression. But we survived. And we have over sixty-six years of combined mental health experience to show for it.

Perhaps now you'll understand why we have such an extensively scientific background for two seemingly spiritual chicks. Growing up, we needed a systematically organized, concrete body of knowledge on any subject, condition, or situation before we could consider it as *truth*. We didn't trust the universe; we didn't trust our spirituality; we didn't trust that good things could come to us. Instead, we took the educational and seemingly safest route. And therein lies the endless road of scientific education.

Many things have changed since then, for better or worse (well, an ongoing commute between the two, really). We are sporting new leases on life as we navigate the unknown with limitless horsepower, accelerating along the road to *happiness*.

Enter …Therapy Twins®

Get in line for the ride of your life. Don't wait as long as we did to strap yourself in and be the change you want to see. You may not like the rules of engagement. We hated them. If we didn't get invited to "the meeting" to make rules, we didn't follow them. But you'll love removing the chains. Oops, the roadblocks.

Instinctively frightened of eighteen-wheelers, we avoided them like the plague as our minds quickly ran reruns of the glass half-empty scenarios. We were full of fear. We didn't know back then that science would prove the *mind* is the steering wheel of the brain.

The Mind Is the Steering Wheel of the Brain

"Everyone thinks of changing the world,
but no one thinks of changing himself."
—Leo Tolstoy

Either we didn't get it, or it was too fucking hard. How could we change when every part of our lives—especially our thoughts—mimicked an idling car?

It's no wonder the first half of our lives was pretty negative. And negative things just kept coming. We didn't realize the roles we were playing in the production of our minds. Anything to keep that applause coming. We were Academy Award winners at "poor me," and queens of sarcasm, resentment, and anger. And fear. Let's not forget about fear. Ahh, United we suffer!

Who would have guessed that your thoughts could be a lie? Investigate and challenge them. Hire a private detective if needed. The brain you're born with doesn't have to be the one you live with all your life. Just like you choose to landscape your property or your body hair, remove a stain from your favorite shirt, remodel your Harley, or purposely rip a pair of jeans to make them stylish, if you don't like where you are you can change it!

You are not a tree, although you may feel like one. We aren't putting you down; we were once trees deeply rooted in patterns of stagnation, like members of a chain gang. We get it; change can be scary, and it often happens slowly. What a bummer! How boring and frankly, unsettling. It would be so much friendlier if it happened quickly. Don't you agree? So read on to make change happen pronto!

What we didn't get for a long time was if you make a conscious choice to change your thoughts about a situation or yourself, you've just flipped a switch. That's great, right? You might have been stuck in traffic for hours, but don't worry. Once you've flipped that switch, there will be movement. The freeway is now open.

So if you find yourself in a gridlock, traffic jam or rush hour take a moment to listen to your thoughts and feelings, and then think again. If they are in any way negative, ask yourself as many times as it takes, how's that working for me? Just as a pathological liar believes his or her lies as truth, you can, too, positive or negative. Your words and thoughts are boomerangs … your choice. At any given moment, fill a glass halfway with water. Now try to convince yourself that it's not only half empty, but it's half full as well. Both are true. But which will you choose? Remember, *the mind is the steering wheel of the brain.*

We think now is the time to throw in the definition and breakdown of a really big word: "neuroplasticity." *Neuro* refers to the brain, and *plasticity* describes the ability to change. So there you have it; not brain freeze but brain change! Think about that. In other words, the placebo effect. The placebo effect occurs when one has a response when given a neutral treatment. The mere belief that one received a medication, for example, causes a physiological change; be it positive or negative.

So choose your thoughts, and your mind will obey. Seem paralyzing and confusing? We know this sounds like a bunch of bullshit, so let's rewind for a moment.

We grew up listening to Muhammed Ali tell the world, "I'm the greatest," and Dr. Seuss told us, "You have brains in your head. You have feet in your shoes. You can steer yourself in any direction you choose" Clearly we weren't listening. How about you?

Throwback to the eighties, when Joan's crippling anxiety echoed fear around every corner, causing her to stop driving. She pretty much expected Jane to be a chauffeur. Jane, tired of driving, decided to help Joan change her behavior rather than challenge that avalanche of fear stored in her memory banks since birth. We don't recommend you try this technique. Ever. By bringing the car to a screeching halt on a busy three-lane highway, Jane gave Joan the choice that if she wanted to see Mommy or Daddy, she had to drive. Even though it required another shower that day, Joan was grateful. She was driving again, which led to a shift in her thinking about driving. Imagine that we began to realize if it's too hard to challenge a thought, begin with changing a behavior. Today, driving a stick shift, no less, happens to be one of Joan's favorite pastimes.

Objects in Mirror Are Closer than They Appear

"No amount of guilt can change the past, and no amount of worrying can change the future".
—Umar Ibnal-khattaab

By definition, post-traumatic stress disorder (PTSD) occurs when you've been a victim of, experienced, or witnessed a traumatic event. Untreated or poorly treated, PTSD symptoms will most certainly lead to anxiety and depression. Basically, anxiety and depression are like siblings. Both are there, one just having more horsepower than the other.

While waiting for her ride, Joan was violently beaten and mugged at age eighteen in Poughkeepsie. Winded, after being hit in the chest, she couldn't yell for help. After helplessly being robbed of both her saddle bag and her innocence, she crawled into the bushes, to hide, fearfully waiting for her ride. Call for help? Nope, she no longer had a dime for the nearby phone booth.

A young man finally walked by. Joan leapt and clung to him, still speechless, until her ride came. For how long is not nearly as important to note as the time it took for her to let go of the lingering fear, pain, and anger.

As if that wasn't enough, in 1985, Joan was sexually assaulted in her family home. Afterward, she exhibited classic rape-victim symptoms, including sitting on the shower floor for long periods while the water rolled upon her, bathing three or more times a day, and using a scrub brush—because the washcloth certainly wasn't enough—to wash her skin until it was excoriated.

Joan experienced the most common symptoms, such as flashbacks, illusions, exaggerated startle reflex, hypervigilance, extreme anxiety, violent outbursts, volatile relationships, and insomnia to name a few (and one that has yet to make it to the DSM-V).

Visual and auditory illusions, for example, were a regular part of Joan's daily existence. She often caught a glimpse of something out of the corner of her eye. Whether it was a piece of hair, a spot on the wall, or merely her eyeglasses. Because of her exaggerated startle reflex, she would jump as if it were a shadow of someone or a bug on the wall. She also heard her name being called when no one was there. That's the one that needs to be added to the DSM! Unfortunately, her symptoms didn't lead Joan to treatment for another ten years.

Jane, on the other hand, didn't realize she also had PTSD. Her symptoms were often clumped together in a diagnosis of depression and anxiety as her symptoms weren't those typical of someone with PTSD. Jane's symptoms included a history of impulsivity and reckless behaviors. You know, when you are finally motivated to leave the house or your bed and walk into an expensive boutique. You have a credit card that happens to have lots of available credit. It wasn't unusual for Jane to charge upwards of $1,000 in under an hour. Jane also had a feeling of detachment from the world around her, difficulty experiencing positive emotions, a delayed startle, flashbacks and of course, insomnia. Her admission to more reckless behaviors is available upon request.

Jane's first clue that something might be wrong occurred on receiving her fifth-grade school photo. After one look at the picture, Daddy responded, "Jane, if you don't start smiling, Mom and I aren't going to pay for these pictures anymore."

Around the tiny age of two, Jane remembers, like a brief video, standing in the second-floor hallway. Mommy was busy in the kitchen, talking with her sisters, and in the other direction was a long staircase. Jane knew her diaper needed changing and remembers assessing both directions. Story has it that she fell down the stairs, requiring stitches in her chin. Jane still wonders if she deliberately threw herself down the stairs to avoid the potential for feeling the abominable sense of shame.

After the fall downstairs, Jane knew of nothing else but ample fear and anxiety as a child, which was masked on and off by severe depression. Completely unaware of this, Jane moved through life experiences almost dissociating, unaware of her feelings. She only knew the sadness with which she awoke each morning and feelings of not wanting to be of this earth.

Therapy Twins® tried to get help here and there through therapy and a myriad of natural remedies and pharmaceuticals. For them, however, it wasn't until they nurtured their bodies, minds, and spirits that something clicked. Kind of like driving your new car for the first time and feeling, *Oh, the possibilities ahead.*

"Life is a balance of holding on and letting go."
—Rumi

History repeats itself unless something changes. What you put out—good or bad—returns to you, whether you think you've summoned it or not. Jane could have continued playing the tragic violin, depressed and isolated. But it became exhausting and definitely wasn't working in her favor, so she chose to do something about it. Not! Joan could have continued living in a horror flick, frightened to death, getting kicked out of public places and family gatherings, tired of being easily agitated, going from zero to sixty in 2.2 seconds. Also exhausted, she finally did something about it. Not!

So did bad things happen to us? Yes. Did we experience trauma? Of course. Did we have a problem with authority?

Definitely. Did we ever get arrested? Absolutely, Get help? God no!

What we didn't know then but can share with you now is that we had choices. Not only did we have choices, but by holding onto the horrors of the past like badges of honor, we unknowingly made the choice to disallow ourselves the joys of living in the present and the notions of having glorious futures.

You might be thinking, *but my past made me who I am!* And you'd be correct. We aren't saying to let go of your memories; we're sure they make for great conversations. But how can we live in the present if we're letting our pasts govern our lives? One foot in yesterday and one in tomorrow make for a guaranteed twilight zone existence.

It got so bad that Jane often thought the hottest guys in the bar were approaching to hit on her. In truth, they just leaned in far enough to ask, "Is it really that bad?"

Joan's temper got so bad that she was nicknamed "Matilda"—not after the French doll, but for a vengeful spirit in a popular thriller who takes on the form of the Tooth Fairy, not leaving coins in exchange for teeth, but leaving havoc! (Well, in the movie, Fairy Godmother killed the children, but Joan wasn't that bad.)

Negative things just kept happening to us. We just didn't realize the roles we played in our own movies to keep the applause coming. Say what? Remember, whether negative or positive, thoughts become reality, so if you choose the negative ones, your reality will mirror negative experiences. Another way of saying it is that your thoughts—and equally important, the feelings behind them—offer you a road trip with an exit to paradise or the twilight zone. The choice of which off-ramp you take is yours as the mind is the steering wheel of the brain. This is the moment to leave old lies in the rearview mirror and embrace the new you. Put your hands on ten and two, and drive.

Be kind to yourself. Allow yourself to choose some tip-top thoughts that will make a shift in your reality that mirrors more positive experiences. Still confused? Go back to Mohammad Ali and Dr. Seuss. If that's too hard right now, think about what President Teddy Roosevelt said: "Believe you can and you are halfway there."

Let's start doubting our negative views of our lives and ourselves and instead choose different roads, paths, trails and expeditions in favor of a better life. We can then choose to be the drivers of our stories and our perceptions. Or, we can choose to remain in park or even drive in reverse.

No matter which choices we make, there will be movement. It's not always positive on the surface—even if you can't see or feel it. Why not choose acceleration and positive free will to maximize desired outcomes; rather than idling or driving miserably in reverse. Again, the choice is yours, it's really always been yours.

Think about a baby who is smiling at everything new, until they are taught negative emotions…fear, anger, horror, guilt and shame. Unfortunately, Therapy Twins® were bred to utilize their five senses as

1. Hear the negativity.
2. See the horror.
3. Touch the gloom.
4. Smell the fear.
5. Taste the bitterness.

But Therapy Twins® give you the green light to

1. Hear the positivity.
2. See the beauty.
3. Touch the happiness.
4. Smell the confidence.
5. Taste the sweetness.

Practice living in the present moment…a lot! Worship your five senses for at least five minutes a day. Really notice the gift in what each one offers in that instance.

Accept it as perfect for *now* because living in the past fuels your sadness, and living in the future ignites anxiety. Remember, not making a choice turns out to be a choice. Making the same mistake twice or three times happens to be a decision. Darn it!

Therapy Twins® give you the green light to recall repeatedly that gratitude is the greatest driver of a grounded life.

Evolutionary Detours

"Everybody's talking at me, can't hear the word they're sayin', only the echoes of my mind."
—Harry Nilsson

Subconscious, selective listening. If you can believe it, this is how we began primitive coping styles. Clearly, we weren't listening to our higher selves because the echoes of our minds reverberated louder than the words of our family, friends, teachers, mentors, textbooks, or self-help *anything*. Still resistant to change, we used immature coping skills with ease since mature ones require, you know, looking *honestly* at yourself and your part in the issue at hand. Accountability? Fuck *that* sideways!

If you're anything like us (or the echoes of our past), change happened slowly, or not at all. Sloths were our inspiration, and shortcuts, or evolutionary detours—were always welcomed. The pursuit of emotional growth and positive change was further hindered by the fact that we were identical twins, idling by, leaning on each other like a pair of tires on the same truck. *Jackknife*!

Fast forward to the 90's when Jane got a divorce and moved back to Connecticut, it seemed all too arduous for Jane to make friends. Her mind echoed the false belief that no one wants to be friends with a negative Nellie. So what's the use of trying?

The most obvious detour in this situation? Jane decided to adopt Joan's friends as her own. Now how easy was that? Insta-friends by association, and she wouldn't have to change a thing. She could go on believing her old negative Nellie story and still achieve the desired outcome. *Genius!* It took her years before she was comfortable befriending anyone on her own.

Joan, holding a 1.9 GPA in college and repeatedly threatened with being kicked out of the dorms, believed she had a choice to make. She could struggle to become a mere college dropout (with many failed alternative career attempts, like becoming a pilot). Or she could attempt to follow in Jane's footsteps by becoming a registered nurse who could afford to buy fantastic shoes on a regular basis. Of course, this seemed like a no-brainer.

Since Joan was frightened to death of the academic process and even more so at the notion of failing, Jane volunteered to go on the college interview for her. After all, she was already a nurse. Jane slam-dunked the interview, and Joan was accepted to Quinnipiac College (please keep that part between us!). Joan repaid the favor after the birth of Jane's son. Yup, Jane got it ... postpartum depression. What a surprise! One more plus of being an identical twin—Joan's happy face became the surrogate mom.

We kept hearing (or selectively *not* hearing, whatever the case may be) that happiness is a journey, and you make your own. *Ugh! Really?* Couldn't it just *happen?* Couldn't we just pass the buck? Darn it! We had to actually *do* something?

After many years of employing the definition of insanity—trying the same thing over and over and expecting different results we finally succumbed to the idea that maybe our coping mechanisms weren't working for us but against us. Maybe we weren't the brilliant, emotionally evolved individuals we believed ourselves to be. Perhaps it was time we embarked on one of those metaphorical road trips.

We could probably supply a dozen examples to drive this point home. But we'll spare you the details for now in hopes that you're beginning to understand you don't have to do it alone. It's okay to need some help, and sometimes you must ask. And sometimes you just must get behind the wheel.

You have the green light from Therapy Twins® to make *any* change, even if it's simply your new mantra, "I'm ready to change."

The Remote Starter

"Life is one big road with lots of signs.
So when you're riding through the ruts, don't
complicate your mind. Flee from hate, mischief,
and jealousy. Don't bury your thoughts, put
your vision to reality. Wake up and live!"
—Bob Marley

Also known as life, there are three major areas from which our echoes, negative or positive, reverberate:

1. Home
2. Work
3. Relationships

The first and third seemed far too difficult, so we did those last. Work seemed to be the easiest because we both achieved higher education first. After all, books are far easier to deal with than humans, including *ourselves*.

Before really delving into our personal relationships (because strangers are way easier to deal with than family), we decided to conduct a change in thought and behavior experiment, using road rage as the subject.

Jane decided to change how she perceived "bad" drivers by joyfully making up stories. For example, "He cut me off 'cause he had to get to the hospital," or, "He's blowing his horn at me because if he's late for work one more time, he'll be suspended," and, "He's riding my bumper because he was a race car driver in a previous life."

If stuck in a traffic jam, Jane eventually decided the universe must want her to slow down for some reason. It was usually in those moments she'd have her greatest epiphanies.

Joan noticed that instead of cursing at them, her road rage was pacified by imagining the driver naked on the side of the road in a Matchbox version of his or her car. When she was in a hurry, rather than honk the horn when someone was driving slowly ahead of her, she'd exclaim, "Wow, I have a super-citizen in front of me," imagining they were saving her from an accident up ahead. After a few times—well, maybe a few hundred times—Joan suddenly noticed she no longer felt those twinges of anger resulting from her usual triggers, be they on the road or in day-to-day life.

One day we finally noticed there was no more road rage within or around us. We don't hear blowing horns, smell burning rubber, or shout profanities unless we *choose* to relapse. Some deep shit, huh?

Now we had an incentive to try it in other aspects of our lives. After all, we'd learned by now that whatever we give our attention to, we invite into our experience, whether we mean to or not.

So once again, let's clarify. We grew up with Mohammad Ali on TV because our dad loved him. When he made his famous proclamation, "I am the greatest," we believed him. Didn't you? What you might not know is Ali began saying, "I am the greatest," prior to his first fight for the World Heavyweight Championship title, with 7:1 odds against him.

Jane began practicing a glass half full approach in her interactions and viewing others through compassionate eyes. Joan was reduced to listening to self-help CDs while she slept for if she were awake, she'd just assault the narrator with defiant profanities.

Therapy Twins® give you the green light to fake it till you make it.

Shifting

"The wheel turns. Nothing is ever new."
—Sherlock Holmes
(From: A *Scandal in Belgravia*)

One day Mommy asked Joan, "Why do you worry so much? What do you have to be so nervous about?"

Joan replied, "I don't need anything to worry about. I can just make something up!"

Do you see how an old pattern can become part of your identity? It's important to ask yourself, "How's this working for me?" After all, nothing changes until it changes.

An even bigger question to ask ourselves after something traumatic has happened to us or someone we love is, "How does one let go?" Or, "How does forgiveness work?" The answer: *practice.* The hardest idea to swallow is that people tend to believe forgiveness is a means by which to minimize the offense or simply suggest that something didn't happen.

We're here to validate for you that it *did* happen. We know it happened, and with all the compassion in our hearts, we're sorry it happened. We're also here to warn you that you may never get an apology. In fact, if you have, you might feel it didn't do you any good. And you could be right. Well, it often doesn't because the work—or more important, the *healing*—is inside you.

Here are some exercises for you to try. Please review each one. Choose what works for you. Try not to immediately discount any of them as they are what helped us in our journeys. We still find them exponentially helpful.

Techniques for Downshifting and Letting Go

Every experience—and we mean *every* experience—has brought us to where we are today. So we implore you to review all your positive experiences and begin actively thanking the Universe, God, the Angels, Mother Nature or the big Cypress tree out front for the experiences before you attempt to review and be grateful for your *upsetting experiences*, no matter how insignificant or massive you think they may be. When you have mastered your gratefullness for all that is *good* Therapy Twins® feel you are ready to begin letting some of that old negative shit go. How, you ask? Pick one or more of these exercises to help tune up your engine and master being grateful for all that was/is negative in your life!

Gratitude

If you believe in gratitude-directed thinking or manifestation (which by now we hope you do), fill in the blank.

> Thank you, _____ (*insert individual's name or situation here),* for that negative experience. I'd like to return it to you with Love for your own emotional healing. I give thanks.

(*Do not, under any circumstances, thank the individual directly because you may get fired, arrested or ostracized! Remember, this is a private exercise for your own personal *healing.*

Say or write this three times. We recommend writing as we feel it somehow carries more power when we must physically construct the words and see them staring back at us on a page. If you struggle with the word "love," as

Joan has for many years (although she is coming to terms with that), you can replace it with "kindness."

This exercise has always worked best for us at the end of the day, but choose your best time according to your own comfort level.

If you believe in past lives, this wording may feel more suitable.

> Thank you, _____, for that negative experience because what you are doing to me in this life, I may have done to you in a past life. I forgive you as I forgive myself. and I refuse to continue the negative experience.

Once again, write this three times, following up with, "I give thanks."

There's Movement in Coming to a Full Stop

Put another way, silence can be a complete sentence. You aren't required to respond to everything. Borrow some duct tape! Some things really are better left unsaid, especially unsolicited advice or a strong opinion. No one is listening anyway. Just kidding. Not about the duct tape, though!

Crank Up the Volume

Music, on the other hand, can change your thoughts almost immediately, so choose wisely. Research shows that listening to soothing or uplifting beats releases dopamine, one of the brain's happy chemicals that motivate us to take action toward our desires, goals, and needs.

Therapy Twins® say, "The louder the better."

Check the Motivations behind Your Thoughts and Behaviors

And then check them again. Therapy Twins® believe positive motivations like love and kindness, have better outcomes than negative ones, such as hurt and anger. Scientists have known since the late 1800s that the heart sends far more signals to the brain than vice versa. These signals have profound effects and connections to both the primitive and sophisticated areas of the brain responsible for emotions, perceptions, and thoughts.

You might want to take a seat now. Yes, the *heart* is an amazing information-processing and sensory system; it's like a living computer. The circuitry of the *heart computer* enables this precious organ to learn, remember, and make decisions completely independent of the *brain*.

We told you the mind is the steering wheel of the brain. So now do you see how important it is to have more positive thoughts than negative ones?

Therapy Twins® give you the green light to heal your *Heart*.

Forgiveness Is the New F Word

"To forgive is to set a prisoner free and discover that the prisoner was you". (Lewis B. Smedes)

Forgiveness doesn't mean it didn't happen or it was okay. It wasn't okay. Take back your power and free yourself from the grips of the past. Sounds confusing? It is … and hard! If you think you're unable to forgive, you're wrong. Simply change the words and perceptions. How about this? Pay more attention to your resiliency and ability to survive something so tragic! Spend more time thinking about your positive traits that got you through it. There, you've just taken back your power and started training your brain. Remember neuroplasticity? You can do it. We're cheering you on! Break those chains, and stop believing old, sticky, heavy, painful ways of thinking.

> Change the way you usually react or respond to someone, and it may change his or her response. Therapy Twins call this exercise human manipulation.

> Stop saying unkind words about yourself or others. When you have an unkind thought, remember that everything people say and do is all about them, including you!

"What Does That Mean?" You Might Ask

Begin thinking about all the things you've said to or about others. Pay close attention to the most common ones … You know, "Why are you so angry?" "You're always late." "He's so selfish." "She thinks she's all that."

Now for the awkward part. Remember, everything you say is really all about you. Wherever the words "you," "he," "she," "they," and so on appear, insert "I" or "I am." Yup, that's right: "I'm so angry." "I'm always late"; "I'm so selfish"; "I think I'm all that." You may say, "I'm never late." Well, maybe you aren't late for work or social gatherings, but you may be late in returning phone calls or paying a bill. How about, "I'm not the angry one"? Well, maybe you're angry about social injustices, life not been fair, or that others don't adopt or agree with your point of view. "I'm right, *right?*"

This exercise can be fun if you let it be. It is one of the easiest ways to figure out your emotions, become more self aware and realize that oh so provocative lesson …"everything you say and do is really all about you!" What an epiphany! It only took us 50 years! How about you? Always remember …

> "Everything you've ever wanted is on the
> other side of fear" George Addair

We hope you enjoyed the ride as much as we did! We promised a "smooth ride"…if you felt speed bumps, please return to Chapter 1!!

Therapy Twins® give you the green light to Love more and *fear* less….and remember….*We are all in this journey together*!

Therapy Twins are mental health experts with more than 66 years of combined experience. Both are graduates of Columbia University with masters of science degrees in psychiatric nursing. They (Jane and Joan) are published in peer-reviewed journals in both the United States and England and have done radio, videos and television programs targeting hot mental health topics. They live in Connecticut with their family.

CPSIA information can be obtained
at www.ICGtesting.com
Printed in the USA
LVOW12s1740060418
572581LV00001B/177/P